£100

t

summersdale

A LITTLE BIT OF GOLFING WIT

Copyright © Summersdale Publishers Ltd, 2010

With text contributed by Aubrey Malone.

All rights reserved.

No part of this book may be reproduced by any means, nor transmitted, nor translated into a machine language, without the written permission of the publishers.

Condition of Sale
This book is sold subject to the condition that it shall not, by way of trade or otherwise, be lent, re-sold, hired out or otherwise circulated in any form of binding or cover other than that in which it is published and without a similar condition including this condition being imposed on the subsequent publisher.

Summersdale Publishers Ltd
46 West Street
Chichester
West Sussex
PO19 1RP
UK

www.summersdale.com

Printed and bound in Great Britain

ISBN: 978-1-84953- 088-0

Disclaimer
Every effort has been made to attribute the quotations in this collection to the correct source. Should there be any omissions or errors in this respect we apologise and shall be pleased to make the appropriate acknowledgements in any future edition.

Substantial discounts on bulk quantities of Summersdale books are available to corporations, professional associations and other organisations. For details contact Summersdale Publishers by telephone: +44 (0) 1243 771107, fax: +44 (0) 1243 786300 or email: nicky@summersdale.com.

A LITTLE BIT OF
Golfing Wit

TOM HAY

Contents

Editor's Note

As Peter Dobereiner once said, 'Everyone gets wounded in a game of golf. The trick is not to bleed.' There can be no denying that, despite all its purported sophistication and gentlemanly conduct, a bad round of golf can be a killer – and while they may not help you get that all-important hole-in-one, this collection of quips and quotes for the golf-obsessed will certainly give you something to laugh about after one too many birdies.

So when it's your turn to buy everyone drinks at the nineteenth, put your best ball forward and dig deep into this little compendium of golfing treasures to find the perfect one-liner for any occasion.

WHAT IS GOLF?

Golf is somewhere between
making love and writing
a poem.
John Updike

Golf is the loneliest of all games, not excluding postal chess.

Peter Dobereiner

The game was invented for simpletons.

Spike Milligan

Golf is a game in which players lie about their scores to people who used to be their friends.

Karen Durasch

Golf was never meant to be an exact science. Einstein was lousy at it.

Bob Toski

Golf is not a funeral, though both can be very sad affairs.

Bernard Darwin

Golf is not a sport. Golf is men
in ugly pants, walking.

Rosie O'Donnell

Golf's not that hard. The ball
doesn't move.

Ted Williams

HIT AND MRS

One of Job's chief trials was that his wife insisted on playing golf with him.

P. G. Wodehouse

Footballers' wives fall out of taxis blathered. The worst a golf wife does is wear an uncoordinated dress.

Shelly Kirkland

Golf wives are more 'Stepford' than 'Footballers''.

Robert O'Byrne

Husband: I got a new set
of clubs for my wife.
Friend: That sounds like
a fair swap.

Bill Wannan

Golf is wrecking my head. Yesterday I kissed my seven-iron goodbye and putted my wife.

Don Rickles

I plan to be a golf widow
next week. I've just
bought the gun.

Joan Rivers

—◆—

Our relationship lasted
longer than either of his
two marriages.

**Nick Faldo's caddy David
Leadbetter, who was sacked
by Faldo after 13 years**

—◆—

You can take a man's wife.
You can even take his wallet.
But never on any account
take his putter.

Archie Compston

My putter worked so well…
I'm going to sleep with it
tonight. My husband will
have to go next door.

Joanne Carner

THE CRUEL GAME

Everyone gets wounded in a
game of golf. The trick is not
to bleed.

Peter Dobereiner

I thought about taking up golf… and then I thought again.

Groucho Marx

Give me a man with big hands, big feet and no brains… I will make a golfer out of him.

Walter Hagen

Golf is the cruellest of
sports… It plays with men
and runs off with the butcher.

Jim Murray

I've never been depressed
enough to take up the game.
Will Rogers

Golf has given me an
understanding of the
futility of life.

Aubrey Eban

You learn a lot about yourself
by playing golf. Unfortunately,
most of it is unprintable.

Burt Lancaster

I've been playing golf for 20 years now and have just made a discovery. I hate it.

Rex Beach

THE NINETEENTH HOLE

If you drink, don't drive.
Don't even putt.
Dean Martin

What scoundrel took the cork
out of my lunch?

**W. C. Fields during a 'snack' break
at the Lakeside Club in LA**

My favourite hole was always
the watering hole.

Ronan Rafferty

First time I played the
Masters… I drank a bottle of
rum… I shot the happiest 83
of my life.

Chi-Chi Rodriguez

Scotland is the birthplace of golf… which may explain why it is also the birthplace of whisky.

Henry Beard

The nineteenth hole is
the only one where players
can have as many shots
as they like.

Louis Safian

GOLF TIPS

The secret of missing a tree is
to aim straight for it.

Michael Green

One may do you good, but if you swallow the whole bottle you'll be lucky to survive.

Harvey Pennick on how golf tips are like aspirin

Never give up a hole. Quitting between tee and green is more habit-forming than drinking highballs before breakfast.

Sam Snead

Never try to keep more than 300 separate thoughts in your mind during your swing.

Henry Beard

Hit it a bloody sight harder!

Ted Ray after a novice asked him how he might get the ball to travel further

Golf should never be played
on any day with a 'y' in it.

Les Dawson

PRACTICE MAKES PERFECT

They call me a natural player.
So why do I have to practise
till my hands bleed?

Seve Ballesteros

I hate practice; my idea
of warming up is a double
egg, sausage, bacon
and fried bread.

Michael Parkinson

Golf teaches us that although practice doesn't always make perfect, no practice always makes us imperfect.

Tom Hartman

I have taught golf at a driving-range… and have seen many people actually practising mistakes.

Mel Flanagan

—•—

I don't practise much these days. At my age, you need to keep all your energy for your actual shots.

Sam Snead at 78

—•—

When Julius Boros putts, you can't tell by looking whether he's… practising or it's fifty grand if he sinks it.

Lee Trevino

LET'S PUTT IT
LIKE THIS

Whoever said putting was
a pleasure obviously never
played golf.

Michael Green

Putt in haste and
repent at leisure.

Gerald Batchelor

I think I know the answer
to your putting problems.
You need to hit the ball
closer to the hole.

**Valerie Hogan to her legendary
husband Ben**

The only time Clayton Heafner could putt was when he got mad enough to hate the ball into the hole.

Cary Middlecoff

There are three things a
man must do alone:
testify, die, and putt.

Bennett Cerf

I was putting like a
lobotomised baboon.

Tony Johnston

I still have the putter with which I missed that two-and-a-half-foot putt to win the Open. It's in two pieces.

Doug Sanders

———•———

Do that again and you'll
wear my putter.

**Bob Shearer to a photographer
who distracted him while playing
a shot in 1975**

———•———

When you're putting badly
you can hear a man jingle two
coins in his pocket 100 yards
away.

Tony Jacklin

To 'put' is to place something somewhere. To 'putt' is to fail to do so.

Gary Koch

❧

Tommy Bolt's putters spent
more time in the air
than Lindberg.

Jimmy Demaret

❧

ER, COME AGAIN?

My fifteen minutes of fame
ran to almost a decade.

Laura Baugh

Seve Ballesteros is relaxed in
an intense sort of way.

Colin Montgomerie

I must play less in order to
prolong my career.

Seve Ballesteros

I would like to thank the press
from the heart of my bottom.

Nick Faldo

Ninety-five per cent of putts
which finish short don't go in.

Robert Green

Nick Faldo this afternoon is all in blue, with a white shirt.

Tony Adamson

❧ ❧

So, Woosie, you're from Wales. What part of Scotland is that?

American journalist to Ian Woosnam during a 1987 press conference

❧ ❧

———•———

Pinero has missed the putt.
I wonder what he's thinking
in Spanish.

Renton Laidlaw

———•———

MAGNIFICENT OBSESSION

Golf is not a relaxation.
Golf is a religion.

Sir Bob Reid

What is love compared to
holing out before
your opponent?

P. G. Wodehouse

Real golfers go to
work to relax.

George Dillon

Golf is my profession.
Show business is just
to pay the green fees.

Bob Hope

Golfers… they only talk
about golf three times a day:
before… while… and after
they've played.

Katharine Whitehorn

You know you're a bit weird
when you ask for *Golf Digest*
bedtime stories at three.

John Ellis

CLOTHES LINES

I'd give up golf if I didn't have
so many sweaters.

Bob Hope

I had to change into brown trousers after playing my first hole at the Masters.

Trevor Homer

The golfing girl of today
should indeed be grateful
that she need not play in
a sailor hat.

Mabel Stringer

I hope you're wearing
that for a bet.

**Colin Montgomerie to
Payne Stewart**

—◆—

I have known girls to become
golfers as an excuse to
wear pink jumpers.

P. G. Wodehouse

—◆—

My God, I've got socks
older than you.

**Lee Trevino to a 27-year-old
opponent**

I was asked to leave my last one because my socks weren't colour coordinated with my umbrella.

Mildred Sassoon on the fussiness of golf clubs

I'll take a two-shot penalty, but I'll be damned if I'm going to play the ball where it lies.

Elaine Johnson after her tee-shot rebounded off a tree and ended up in her bra

WEIGHT WATCHERS

If it wasn't for golf, I'd
probably be the fat lady
in the circus now.

Kathy Whitworth

It takes a lot of guts to play golf… look at Billy Caspar… he has a lot of guts.

Gary Player

I've lost 40 pounds since Christmas – 150 if you include the wife.

David Feherty

Some guys try to shoot their age. Craig Stadler tries to shoot his weight.

Jim Murray

Golf and cricket are the only
two games where you can
actually put on weight
while playing them.

Tommy Docherty

Most of the guys on the tour
are built like truck drivers but
have the touch of hairdressers.

Clayton Heafner

CONUNDRUMS

Why is it called a three-wood
when it's made out of metal?

Ernie Witham

If the universe is finite…
how come golfers never
find all the balls they lose?

Hal Roach

Is it any accident that 'God' comes just before 'golf' in the dictionary?

Dave Allen

If golf is a rich man's game,
how come there are so
many poor players?

Mitch Murray

Do golfers' drives put
them crazy or their putts
drive them crazy?

Valerie Ferguson

One day you play really well
and the next really crap – and
you don't know why.

Patrick Rayner

HERE'S TO THE LOSERS

Few things draw two men
together more than a mutual
inability to play golf.

P. G. Wodehouse

The only thing I ever learned
from losing was that I
don't like it.

Tom Watson

… there are 2,000 different ways you can hit the ball wrong. So far I think I've reached about 1,800.

Dinah Shore

Defeat is worse than death,
because you have to live
with defeat.

Nick Faldo

I play golf like Cinderella.
I never make it to the ball.

Don Rickles

I have often been gratefully
aware of the heroic efforts
of my opponents not to
laugh at me.

Bernard Darwin

I wouldn't know a nine-iron
from a steam iron.

Lise Hand

Show me a good loser and
I'll show you a loser.

Gary Player

Golf.

**Jackie Gleason after being asked
what his handicap was**

❦

The worse you play, the better
you remember the occasional
good shot.

Nubar Gulbenkian

❦

My most notable trait is
snatching defeat out of
the jaws of victory.

Doug Saunders

I played so badly I got a
'get well' card from the
Inland Revenue.

Johnny Miller

I achieved a lot by climbing over 113 golfers. The only problem was that there were 114 ahead of me.

Joanne Carner

CADDYSHACK

The first thing to understand about caddying is that it's not brain surgery. It's much more complicated than that.

Lawrence Donegan

Players make mistakes.
Caddies make blunders.

Jerry Osborne

Divorces between caddies and players are often executed on the spot, and there isn't any alimony.

John O'Reilly

Golfer to caddy after messing up a shot: Golf is a funny old game, innit?
Caddy: The way you play it, it certainly is, sir.

Greg Doherty

❦

Real golfers… never strike a caddy with the driver. The sand wedge is infinitely more effective.

Huxtable Pippey

❦

— · —

I asked Marilyn Monroe if she'd come golfing… 'I can't,' she said, 'I don't even know how to hold the caddy.'

Dean Martin

— · —

SANDBAGGERS

Lawrence of Arabia, Tarbuck
of Las Brisas… when you
speak of sand, we have
been there.

Jimmy Tarbuck

There's no rule against your standing over him and counting his strokes aloud with increasing gusto.

Horace Hutchinson on when your opponent is stuck in a bunker

At my age it's tough trying to get out of the bunkers. I mean after I've hit the ball.

George Burns

I never kick my ball in the
rough or improve my lie in
a sand trap. For that I
have a caddy.

Bob Hope

I call golf 'Connect the
Sand Traps'.

Jack Benny

A sand trap is a deep depression of sand, filled with golfers in deep depressions.

Henry Beard

THE EGOS HAVE LANDED

There are days when you feel you can't miss even when you try to.

Jack Nicklaus

If I didn't sign autographs
while I was walking, I'd never
make my tee-off time.

Colin Montgomerie

❧

I never mis-hit a shot. Every drive was perfect, and every iron. I was in awe of myself.

Greg Norman after winning the British Open

❧

❦

Any time I get ideas above
my station my wife says,
'Put the garbage out.'
Sandy Lyle

❦

If I can hit it I can hole it.

Arnold Palmer

Arnold Palmer doesn't so much walk onto the first tee as climb into it… as though it were a prize ring.

Charles Price

It was so good I could nearly
feel the baby applauding.

**A seven-months-pregnant Donna
White after a good putt**

My driving is so good these days I have to dial the operator long distance after I hit it.

Lee Trevino

—◆—

I always ask my caddy to tell me two things: the yardage, and that I'm the best in the world.

Jack Nicklaus

—◆—

All of us believe that our good shots are the norm, and our bad ones aberrations.

Alec Morrison

One minute it's fear and loathing, but hit a couple of good shots and you feel like God.

Jack Nicholson

COURSES FROM HELL

There's nothing wrong with
St Andrews that a hundred
bulldozers couldn't put right.

Ed Furgol

When the wind blows at
St Andrews, even the
seagulls walk.

Nick Faldo

More players have fantasised about killing me than they have about killing Jack the Ripper.

Course designer Robert Trent Jones, renowned for his 'sadistic' courses

Golf is a cruel game anyway,
so why should I design
courses fairly?

Peter Dye

All Hazeltine needs is eighty acres and some cows.

Dave Hill

LET'S GET PHYSICAL

A true pro always prefers his
golf course to his intercourse.

Conan O'Brien

I wish it had bitten me a little lower down.

David Feherty, whose arm swelled up to twice its normal size after being bitten by a snake at Wentworth

Golf and sex are the only two things you can enjoy without being good at either.

Jim Davidson

Would you say a golfer is a
man who putts it about?

Ben Elton

My wife gave me ten oysters
last night to rouse my passion,
but only nine of them worked.

Lee Trevino

Golf groupies must be
the most passive of any
competitive game. Even chess
fans display greater vivacity.

Robert O'Byrne

THE ICONS

Nick Faldo's idea of
excitement is having his After
Eight mints at 7.30.

Graham Elliot

Arnold Palmer would go for
the flag from the middle of
an alligator's back.

Lee Trevino

John Daly could draw a
crowd in Saskatchewan.

Rocco Mediate

—◆—

Big Four – Palmer, Nicklaus, Player and Trevino. I just want to be the fifth wheel in case somebody gets a flat.

Chi-Chi Rodriguez

—◆—

Maybe I should dye my hair peroxide blonde and call myself The Great White Tadpole.

Ian Woosnam on how he might create a remarkable image for himself

In the real world a bad week
is waking up and finding
you're a steelworker
in Scunthorpe.

Nick Faldo

—◆—

Jack Nicklaus is a legend
in his spare time.

Tom Watson

—◆—

Tiger Woods has such a lazy
style, last week I caught him
nodding off on his backswing.

Valerie Netter

Seve Ballesteros hits the
ball farther than I go
on my holidays.
Lee Trevino

BYE BYE BIRDIE

I gave up golf for painting
because it takes me
less strokes.

Dwight D. Eisenhower

I know exactly when I want to retire now, but when I reach that time I may not.

Jack Nicklaus

We don't stop playing because we get old. We get old because we stop playing.

Walter Hagen

Men chase golf balls when
they're too old to chase
anything else.

Groucho Marx

When birds flying south
readjust their flight patterns
to let you hit.

**Richard Miziner on the time to
give up golf**

That was a great game
of golf, fellers.

Bing Crosby's reputed last words

I'm fed up of retired tennis players taking up golf. When I retire, I'm going to take up tennis.

Jimmy Demaret

My boss told me I needed
to de-stress myself… he
suggested golf… a very wise
suggestion. I gave it up.

Ben Cabot

Have you enjoyed this book? If so,
why not write a review on your
favourite website?

Thanks very much for buying this
Summersdale book.

www.summersdale.com